THE CONSTITUTION
Understanding America's Founding Document

Michael S. Greve

AEI Press
Washington, D.C.

Distributed by arrangement with the Rowman & Littlefield Publishing Group, 4501 Forbes Boulevard, Suite 200, Lanham, MD 20706. To order call toll free 1-800-462-6420 or 1-717-794-3800.

For all other inquiries please contact AEI Press, 1150 17th Street, N.W., Washington, D.C. 20036 or call 1-800-862-5801.

Greve, Michael S.
  The Constitution : understanding America's founding document / Michael S. Greve.
    pages cm
  ISBN 978-0-8447-7258-5 (pbk.)
  ISBN 0-8447-7258-5 (pbk.)
  ISBN 978-0-8447-7259-2 (ebook)
  ISBN 0-8447-7259-3 (ebook)
  1. Constitutional history--United States--18th century.
  2. United States--History--1783-1815. I. Title.
  KF4541.G75 2013
  342.7302--dc23

THE CONSTITUTION
Understanding America's Founding Document

CONTENTS

ACKNOWLEDGMENTS

For helpful comments on an earlier draft of the book manuscript, I am indebted to John Dinan, Anna Gasaway, Anna Sophia Greve, and Michael Zuckert. Thanks also to Elizabeth DeMeo for her splendid assistance and to Greg Lane and AEI's Values & Capitalism team for capable editorial services and project management.

1

INTRODUCTION

The United States Constitution ranks among the greatest accomplishments of the human spirit. For well over two centuries, it has served as a charter for a free, democratic government, for a country that has risen from a dicey political experiment and agrarian backwater to an economic and political superpower. In the history of the world, there is nothing like it.

There are many fruitful ways of examining the Constitution (see box 1). Historians study the social, political, and economic circumstances that surround the country's founding, as well as the philosophical traditions that influenced the Founding Fathers (for example, John Locke's idea of a "social contract" and Montesquieu's theory of the separation of powers). Lawyers parse the constitutional text and Supreme Court opinions: after all, the Constitution is law, albeit of a special kind. Political scientists, economists, and moral philosophers all have produced an enormous literature on the Constitution. You will find a few of the many terrific books under "Recommended Reading."

Box 1: Read the Constitution

In reading this book, you should keep a copy of the United States Constitution at hand. High-school summaries, snippets from Supreme Court opinions, or vague recollections of "due process" and the like are no substitute for knowledge of the actual text in its entirety.

An indispensable guide to the Constitution is the series of 85 essays called *The Federalist* (or *The Federalist Papers*), authored in 1787–88 by Alexander Hamilton, James Madison, and John Jay under the pen name Publius. To this day, constitutional lawyers and judges cite *The Federalist* as an authoritative commentary on the Constitution. However, Publius provides much more than a lawyerly exposition; he also provides a profound political theory of the Constitution. *The Federalist* is quoted and cited throughout this book. Consider it an invitation to familiarize yourself with the major essays.

This small book, approximately twice the length of the United States Constitution and the Bill of Rights, provides a broader context. It isn't about *what* to think about the Constitution; it is about *how* to think seriously about our constitution and constitutions in general, for example:

- What are constitutions supposed to do, and what can they do? Establish a government for a free society, you might say, and that is not a bad answer. But then China and Cuba have constitutions, and they are hardly free. Conversely, some free countries (England, New Zealand, Israel) had or have no written constitution. What does this tell us?

- The United States Constitution is the oldest existing national constitution in the world. (The average longevity of constitutions around the world is under twenty years.) Why is that? Has the Constitution lasted because our politics have remained democratic, or is it the other way around?

- In 2012, Supreme Court Justice Ruth Bader Ginsburg remarked that no one today would write a constitution the way ours is written. That is surely right; for example, modern constitutions contain many more rights than ours. Why is this? Does it mean that our constitution is outdated and in need of drastic reform?

There are no single "right" answers to these and similar questions. But there are more or less productive ways of thinking about them. This book suggests promising avenues of thought and inquiry. Two of its more provocative thoughts warrant a brief mention up front.

First, the contemporary constitutional debates are preoccupied with constitutional rights and the Supreme Court. Our rights and their judicial protection, the thinking goes, are the essence of constitutional government. That account has some truth to it. However, it leaves out too much. The modern rights-focused and court-centered perspective was emphatically not the founders' viewpoint. Nor does it reflect the way the constitutional order has operated for most of our history. Accordingly, this book starts with a broader perspective—with the political premises and calculations that underpin the Constitution (chapter 2) and with its general principles and architecture (chapters 3–5). Rights and the Supreme Court are best understood within that larger context (chapters 6 and 7).

Second, I hope to impart a deeper appreciation of, and intellectual engagement with, the "miracle" of the Constitutional Convention in Philadelphia in 1787. The convention was a response to a failed political experiment. The Articles of Confederation, under which the states had operated since 1781, had saddled the union with grave political problems—for example, a mountain of public debt at a level that tends to spell public rebellion and the ruin of nations. The founders tackled those problems with boldness and resolve, and they triumphed over vehement opposition. That alone is a stupendous achievement.

More remarkably still, though, the founders went well beyond the immediate problems to an audacious proposition: a free people, they insisted, can establish democratic government not only for themselves but also, as the Constitution's preamble confidently declares, for "Posterity," meaning future generations. At some level, that project seems downright absurd. The founders understood very well that they knew next to nothing about the conditions and problems future generations would encounter. Still, and as if the daunting political problems before them weren't enough, the founders insisted on crafting a grand solution for the long term. Why?

In chapter 2, this book explains why the founders' ambition is, in fact, central to their constitutional project. But it also approaches the question from the opposite, contemporary perspective: why should we pay any heed to a bunch of wigged gentlemen two-plus centuries ago (apart from the bare fact that we happen to live under their constitution)? Chapters 8 and 9 discuss two of the historical experiences that separate us from the founders: the slavery problem, which required a second founding, and the creation of a vast administrative state beyond the founders' wildest imagination. No doubt you can think of other problems that appear to make the founders look naïve or obtuse. They all suggest the question addressed in chapter 10: with all the social, economic, and political change and upheaval over the centuries, what does this ancient document mean to us—and what can we still learn from the founders?

I invite you to consider a strange thought: perhaps the founders understood us better than we understand ourselves. The concluding chapter 11 suggests how and why that might be so. You may eventually reject that unconventional thought. Entertaining it, however, has its own rewards. At a time when our politics seem petty and dispiriting, the founders' boldness is like a breath of fresh air.

2

CONSTITUTIONAL POLITICS

Constitutions aim to do two things. First, they make orderly politics possible: they establish institutions with certain powers, specify decision rules (who gets to do what and how), and so forth. Second, and in the same breath, constitutions seek to discipline politics and to limit government power. It is important to keep this two-sided nature in mind. However, it is not unique to constitutions; it also characterizes many ordinary pieces of legislation. (The Securities Exchange Act and the Affordable Care Act, for example, establish government bodies with copious but limited powers.) So what is special about constitutions?

"Constitutions aim to do two things. First, they make orderly politics possible: they establish institutions with certain powers, specify decision rules (who gets to do what and how), and so forth. Second, and in the same breath, constitutions seek to discipline politics and to limit government power."

Ordinary legislation is enacted by existing democratic governments, under known rules. Constitutions, in contrast, must establish the institutions and the rules of future democratic politics, when the rules of the game are up for grabs and the authority of the decision-making bodies is doubtful. Unlike legislators, then, constitution writers cannot rely on a claim of democratic legitimacy; they have to establish it. How?

REFLECTION AND CHOICE

Classical theorists (foremost John Locke, a British philosopher greatly admired by the founders) captured the predicament in the idea of a preconstitutional "state of nature." In that state, Locke contended, free and equal persons hold broad rights to life, liberty, and property. However, they lack the means of enforcing those rights. Thus, individuals give up some of their personal autonomy and consent to a "social contract." Legitimate government requires unanimous consent: anything else is an act of aggression against dissenters.

The Declaration of Independence powerfully echoes Locke's theory of rights and self-determination. However, the theory was too abstract to be of much use to statesmen who confronted a series of pressing political problems and a hard-fought debate in which victory was uncertain and unanimity an absurd fantasy. Then again, abandoning the Lockean aspiration seems equally problematic. Suppose political leaders manage to improvise a political process and, with luck, create a halfway decent constitution: dissenters will be quick to denounce the process and the product as an elite power grab or as a grubby interest group bargain. How, then, can one generate political legitimacy and stability?

Confronted with that dilemma, the founders sought to rest legitimate government on a special, *constitutional* politics—a step down into the real world from Locke's abstract "state of nature" but still altogether different from mere politicking and compromise. The founders called this mode of politics "reflection and choice." Alexander Hamilton's *Federalist* 1 begins on this note:

> It has been frequently remarked, that it seems to have been reserved to the people of this country to decide, by their conduct and example, the important question, whether societies of men are really capable or not, of establishing good government from reflection and choice, or whether they are forever destined to depend, for their political constitutions, on accident and force.

"Accident and force" are the general predicaments of mankind; reflection and choice are a rare moment of a different, constitutional politics. Even then, Hamilton admits, "ambition, avarice, personal animosity, party opposition, and many other motives" are apt to operate on all sides of the debate. Still, he insists that one can tell "evidence of truth" from narrow interests, an "enlarged" and "comprehensive" view of the subject from partial concerns, and "sedate and candid consideration" from partisan agitation.

How, though, can people act on that broader view? A careful reading of *The Federalist* suggests that constitutional reflection and choice require three conditions: an unambiguous democratic sovereign; a time horizon that combines an intense awareness of the constitutional moment with a very long-term perspective; and control over the constitutional agenda.

WE THE PEOPLE

Constitutional choice presupposes agreement on who is doing the choosing and for whom the choice is being made. In other words, it presupposes the sovereign "we the people" of the Constitution's preamble. (Read it carefully!) If people's loyalties to some other collective entity—a tribe, an organized religion, a preexisting state—run too deep to permit agreement on the "we," one cannot have a constitution that is more than an elite bargain or interest group compromise. By good fortune and "Providence," however, Americans find themselves capable of choosing *as one people*. They are blessed with a favorable geography that provides natural boundaries and a connected country; and, within that connected country,

> a people descended from the same ancestors, speaking the same language, professing the same religion, attached to the same principles of government, very similar in their manners and customs, and who, by their joint counsels, arms and efforts, fighting side by side through a long and bloody war, have nobly established their general liberty and independence. (*Federalist* 2)

This passage is not entirely candid. "The same religion," for example, excludes Catholics and Jews, and Publius obviously skirts the wrenching disagreement over slavery. However, one factor is clearly not overstated—the former British colonists' experience of having fought a common war at great cost. *We* know who we are: we are the people who broke away from their mother country, fought a war, and started the world anew.

THE MOMENT AND THE FUTURE

A constitutional politics of reflection and choice is possible; but it is a rare, unprecedented opportunity "reserved to the people of this country." Moreover, the opportunity is not a permanent condition but a brief moment. One obvious danger is a relapse into anarchy, warfare, and general instability, should the plan of the Constitutional Convention be defeated. Another, more insidious danger is a resumption of short-sighted interest group politics, which cannot produce a legitimate constitution. The people must choose *now*, in the brief historical moment when the war is concluded but still recent. In James Madison's words,

> It is too early for politicians to presume on our forgetting that the public good, the real welfare of the great body of the people, is the supreme object to be pursued; and that no form of government whatever, has any other value, than as may be fitted for the attainment of this object. (*Federalist* 45)

It is too early: the recent Revolutionary War had enlarged people's view of "the public good." But a war also helps expand their time horizon, and this point, too, is crucial to the constitutional project. In the short term, individuals generally know their own strengths and weaknesses, and they will try to rig the rules of the game in their own favor. In contrast, a long time horizon creates uncertainty and, correspondingly, curbs selfish temptations: if you don't know your place at a future table, there is no point in loading the dice. Uncertainty enables the people to consider constitutional rules from the perspective of long-term collective gains rather than from short-term, partial advantage.

The constitutional text reflects this perspective. We the people, declares the preamble, seek to "secure the Blessings of Liberty to ourselves *and our Posterity*."

AGENDA CONTROL

Modern social science has shown, conclusively and unsettlingly, that collective decision-making bodies (such as legislatures) can easily produce outcomes that correspond to nobody's actual preferences. In politics, almost anything can happen unless someone controls the agenda. *The Federalist* was clear-eyed in recognizing the problem and very candid about the need for agenda control.

Federalist 40 mounts a confident defense of the principal constitutional agenda setter, the Philadelphia Convention. It was, Publius writes, "composed of men who possessed the confidence of the people, and many of whom had become highly distinguished by their patriotism, virtue, and wisdom." Those men met "in the mild season of peace, with minds unoccupied by other subjects" and without "any passion, except love for their country."

In strictness, the delegates had been charged with amending the Articles of Confederation, not with writing a whole new constitution. But they had also been charged with rendering the government adequate to the preservation of the union. Having realized that this could not be accomplished through mere amendments, the delegates took the only responsible course of action. Moreover, Madison writes, the delegates deliberated in the anticipation that their plan would be submitted to the people themselves, assembled in state conventions. Popular approbation would "blot out all antecedent errors and irregularities."

Wisely, though, Madison refrains from staking too much on that argument. One obvious difficulty was this: while Article XIII of the Confederation permitted amendment only by unanimous consent, ratification by nine rather than all thirteen states would suffice to carry the Constitution into effect. Putting aside questions of strict legality, the departure from unanimity raises the difficult question of how free the tenth state would really be in saying yes or no to the Constitution. Madison's answer is that the unanimity rule would hold the union hostage to the demands of a single small state. Even the opponents of the Constitution, Madison writes, failed to press the point because they recognized "the absurdity of subjecting the fate of twelve states to the perverseness or corruption of a thirteenth."

A second problem was that the convention, by virtue of having met and submitted a plan, had restricted and biased the constitutional choice: all options except yes or no, including a reform of the Articles of Confederation, were now off the table. On second thought, though, that is a good thing. When great changes are called for, Madison explains, "it is impossible for the people spontaneously and universally to move in concert towards their object," and "it is therefore essential that such changes be instituted by some *informal and unauthorized propositions*, made by some patriotic and respectable citizen, or number of citizens." Moreover, yes or no must be the only options. Suppose there is a third option: if one-third prefers the Constitution, another third reform of the Articles, and another third full autonomy for each state, the wretched status quo would yet prevail. For that reason, Publius denounced the seductive "reform the Articles" option as illusory. For the same reason, the Federalists refused to open the convention's product to preapproval amendments (including a bill of rights), even while promising that the first Congress elected under the new constitution would promptly attend to sensible amendment proposals.

LEGITIMACY

How plausible is *The Federalist*'s theory of constitutional reflection and choice as the basis of legitimate government? I have noted some possible doubts, and one can certainly think of additional objections. By modern standards, the right to vote was quite limited at the time, so how democratic was the enterprise? The Constitutional Convention was hardly representative either of society or of public sentiment: it consisted almost entirely of men of wealth and of "Federalist" supporters of a stronger national government to boot. (Suspicious "Antifederalist" supporters of states' rights, such as Virginia's Patrick Henry, had stayed home.) Moreover, the convention cut its deals in secret. All this may seem to obviate the notion of the Constitution as a compelling constitutional choice.

One can also argue, however, that the founders' idea of constitutional politics was excessively ambitious. It is very difficult to show that democratic constitutional choice is possible *at all* and more difficult yet to exercise it. As James Wilson, a leading Federalist, reminded the members of Pennsylvania's ratifying convention, it had never been done in 6,000 years. Moreover, experience since confirms the unique nature of the founders' experiment. Constitutions have emerged from defeat and military occupation (as in Germany and Japan); from arduous negotiations and compromises among political elites; from the breakup of colonial empires; and from revolutions as well as gradual processes of constitutionalization (as in New Zealand and Israel). Some of those constitutions have produced stable liberal democracies. However, it is next to impossible to identify an instance of a constitutional politics that rivals America's in intellectual depth or civic engagement. There are no *Federalist Papers* in any other country's history.

Nor is this surprising. Nations in ruins and countries that are divided by ethnic or religious conflict cannot aspire to "reflection and choice"; their more modest objective must be a compromise that allows them to stop the bloodshed and move on. Even modern democratic societies, operating under more favorable circumstances, cannot easily replicate America's constitutional experience. For example, their deliberations will be dominated by political parties (which the founders loathed), and no modern-day convention would be allowed to proceed in secret. A politics of reflection and choice may yet be possible, but it would have to look very different.

All this suggests that the founders were right to emphasize the exceptional nature of their constitutional moment. It is important to recognize the point, because the Constitution's politics bear on its structure.

3

CONSTITUTIONAL PRINCIPLES AND STRUCTURE

"Reflection and choice" legitimate constitutional government. But they also push toward a particular kind of institutional solution. That solution encompasses five central structural principles: written-ness, minimalism, rigidity, decision rules (rather than distribution rules), and institutional competition. This chapter discusses the first four principles. The competition principle is discussed in chapter 4.

WRITTEN-NESS

Constitution can mean a country's entrenched political customs and institutions (much as we speak of an athlete with a "healthy constitution"). A *written* constitution, in contrast, is a break with the past and an act of will. It signals a new beginning: "Henceforth, this is how we will govern our common affairs."

The famous first words of the preamble boldly and confidently identify the author: "We the people of the United States."[1] The preamble then states the

---

[1] Note that the preamble, unlike the Declaration of Independence and the vast majority of state constitutions then and now, does not mention God or a "Creator." The most likely explanation for this conspicuous omission is the authors' intention to signal that for constitutional purposes, there is only one sovereign: We.

general ends for which "we" "ordain and establish" the Constitution (there are six of them), and it states for whom "we" do so: "ourselves and our Posterity." Because the Constitution is written, posterity can look it up. It is written *so that* posterity can look it up.

The Constitution is also written in a particular way. After the short preamble, the operative provisions are all about powers and procedures. For inspirational language, you will have to look elsewhere. However, the Constitution is not written in legalese either. It contains some words and phrases, often borrowed from the British courts' common law, that carry very specific connotations, such as *habeas corpus*. And it contains a few terms of art ("letters of marque and reprisal": you will have to google them). So far as possible, however, the Constitution is written in words that are understandable to ordinary readers. It is addressed not to populist moralizers or a priestly elite of lawyers but to sober, grown-up citizens who demand to know what their elected and appointed officials can and cannot do.

MINIMALISM

The founders wrote a formal legal text—but they did not write at great length. The Constitution is curiously silent about matters that are often regulated in great detail in modern constitutions.

For example, it says little about citizenship and nothing about political parties or voting rights. (Your free, fair, and secret ballot is a product of our political history, not of the constitutional text.) The Constitution says nothing about education, the environment, infrastructure, or the media. In comparison to modern constitutions, our rights catalogue is skimpy even if you include the Bill of Rights and the Civil War Amendments (the Thirteenth, Fourteenth, and Fifteenth).

It may seem tempting to attribute the Constitution's minimalism to the founders' ignorance of the problems and conditions of our modern, complex, (post-) industrial, high-tech society. This assumption, though, is a bad mistake. Of course, the founders had no inkling of global warming, the Internet, or government-subsidized health care. However, the Constitution also fails to mention matters that the founders did consider, such as infrastructure improvement and education. While the founders deemed those questions important, few thought that they belonged in the Constitution. Two reasons account for the minimalism.

First, the founders recognized that their ambition to produce democratic, limited, stable government cut against any attempt to settle policy disagreements through the Constitution. Divergent and deeply held opinions over public education, the environment, or the death penalty and abortion might undermine the effort to find a constitutional consensus. Second, the founders knew that no one could know what posterity's society would look like and what problems it might pose. Precisely because you don't know, you don't want to tailor the Constitution to current social problems.

Note, though, that constitutional minimalism requires a great deal. First, it requires preexisting habits and institutions that work tolerably well and toward constitutional ends. For example, the founders built on a common law of property, contract, tort, and much else that ordered private markets and relations, along with state courts and juries. Second, constitutional minimalism requires a bold confidence: *we can order our public affairs in the course of ordinary democratic politics, provided we get the basic rules and institutions right*. A constitution for a society that lacks either of those conditions would look, and would have to look, very different.

RIGIDITY

The Constitution's basic arrangements are not easily changed, and its pronounced silences on matters of grave public import are not easily filled: the oldest national constitution in the world is also among the hardest to change by formal amendment. Article V provides for several means of amendment.

> *"The Constitution is rigid for the same reason that it is written and minimalist: it is supposed to last."*

All of them are arduous and require extraordinary majorities.

Scholars and political leaders have often argued, not entirely without reason, that the amendment process is *too* hard. In particular, the requirement that three-fourths of states must consent raises the distinct possibility that a very small minority, composed of razor-thin majorities in small states, may block amendments that are favored by a vast majority of citizens. Sensible arguments along these lines, however, will respect the unmistakable precept that amendments *should* be hard to enact. A mutable constitution, James Madison noted, can never earn "that veneration which time bestows on every thing" (*Federalist* 49). The Constitution is rigid for the same reason that it is written and minimalist: it is supposed to last.

DECISION RULES

Constitutional minimalism goes hand in hand with a firm preference for decision rules, as opposed to *distribution rules* (see box 2). To illustrate the difference: the United States Constitution permits both states and the federal government to tax anyone and anything they want, subject only to a few specified prohibitions and qualifications. (Go look them up!) That is a set of decision rules. Alternatively, a constitution could specify the distribution of revenue between states and the federal government, as well as among states. Many federal constitutions embody such a distributive arrangement. Ours, to repeat, does not: its decision rules govern regardless of the outcomes. In fact, with one glaring exception (the slavery bargain, discussed in chapter 8), the United States Constitution distributes nothing at all except seats in the House of Representatives in accordance with the census.

Box 2: Principles and Politics
The distinction between decision rules and distributions is not the same as a distinction between "high principle" and "lousy compromise."

Distribution rules may embody high-toned principles ("to each in accordance with his need"). Conversely, the United States Constitution's decision rules embody a slew of political compromises—some ingenious, others not so much. The most famous of those compromises, the deal between small and big states on the mode of representation in the House and Senate, did not leave the Constitution's proponents very happy. (*The Federalist* defends the principle of state equality in the Senate on pragmatic grounds and as a necessary concession to small states, but never on principle.) Similarly, the executive emerged as a compromise among delegates who had no very clear idea of what they were doing.

All those compromises, however, are still decision rules, not compromises that attempt to "freeze" a preconceived distribution of entitlements. That sort of compromise is alien to the Constitution, with one profoundly embarrassing exception discussed in chapter 8: the compromise on slavery.

A preference for decision rules, like minimalism, is closely tied both to a desire to generate broad consensus and to the need for constitutional stability. In general, it is easier to reach agreement on decision rules than on distributive rules. Moreover, a distribution rule cannot be anything but a compromise among rival groups (interests, states, or political elites). If the rule is tolerably fair and the parties are in a conciliatory mood, it may represent a "consensus" of sorts. However, that consensus will prove only as stable as the underlying economic conditions and distribution of political forces. Settle for a consensus of that sort in your constitution, and you have saddled posterity with a constitution in need of permanent revision.

4

COMPETITION

Recall the constitutional objective: democratic, limited, stable government. But how is a constitution—words on paper—going to achieve that objective? Madison suggests the answer in a famous passage in *Federalist* 51:

> In framing a government which is to be administered by men over men, the great difficulty lies in this: you must first enable the government to control the governed; and in the next place oblige it to control itself. A dependence on the people is, no doubt, the primary control on the government; but experience has taught mankind the necessity of auxiliary precautions.

"Dependence on the people"—representative democracy or, in the founders' parlance, "republican government"—is an indispensable safeguard against abuse. Every branch of government must derive its powers, ultimately, from the people. But a dependence on the people is also dangerous: the people may turn out to be a self-interested, rapacious majority. Thus, one must "oblige government to control itself" by means of additional, "auxiliary" precautions. What are they?

The common, modern-day answer is rights. Constitutions must be democratic (the more democratic, the better). And to prevent abuse, we establish rights that hold good against impassioned majorities and the governments they may elect. However, that is not the founders' answer; to overstate the case a bit, it is the answer they *rejected*.

On one side, the founders were deeply suspicious of "democracy" in the sense of direct popular participation.[2] On the other side, *The Federalist* dismissed rights as an unreliable "parchment barrier." Instead, the Constitution seeks to establish "auxiliary precautions" on a principle of *institutional competition*.

The founders' skepticism of direct democracy and of rights does not reflect an aristocratic distaste for popular sovereignty or a blanket hostility to rights claims. (It would be very odd to find such dispositions among men who had fought and sacrificed for the principles of the Declaration of Independence.) Rather, the founders' positions reflect a hard-headed realism about what a constitution can and cannot do. The Founders

---

[2] Note, for example, that the United States Constitution, unlike many state constitutions, contains no mechanism for an initiative or a referendum. Instead, the founders relied on representation and "the total exclusion of the people, in their collective capacity" from governmental decisions as a means of blocking democratic excess and of refining political deliberation.

thought that no constitution, least of all a rights-based constitution, can do much to control the people themselves: when a determined mob wants to trample a minority underfoot, it will not let lofty rights declarations get in the way. What a constitution can and must do is to control the *people's agents*—that is, their representatives.

The way to accomplish this end is to divide popular sovereignty among the agents to whom it is delegated and to place those agents in competition for power. This is what Madison means by "auxiliary precautions." His two principal precautions are (1) the "extended republic" and (2) government structure, or "checks and balances."

THE EXTENDED REPUBLIC

In the famous *Federalist* 10, Madison argued—contrary to conventional wisdom at the time—that people's rights would be safer in a large, "extended" republic than in a smaller political system. Within the states, he argued, citizens will be at the mercy of "factions"—that is, "a number of citizens, whether amounting to a majority or a minority of the whole, who are united and actuated by some common impulse of passion, or of interest, adverse to the rights of other citizens, or to the permanent and aggregate interests of the community." Small republics will tend to feature a small number of factions, over a narrow range, which will easily "concert and carry into effect schemes of oppression." An extended sphere mitigates the danger in three ways. First, the larger size of electoral districts will tend to produce better, more public-spirited legislators. Second, a bigger playing field increases the range and number of interests, thus making majorities less likely. Third, the greater range of interests will make factional self-dealing more difficult. The high costs of transacting legislative business will protect "the rights of other citizens" and "the permanent and aggregate interests of the community."

Federalist 10 is devoted to competition as a means of protecting the rights of citizens. *Federalist* 51 acknowledges that the protection of rights is a necessary but not a sufficient condition of good government: at the end of the day, government must legislate and produce order. Madison argues that, in the extended republic, "a coalition of a majority of the whole society could seldom take place upon any other principles, than those of justice and the general good." Thus, political competition is expected to do two things: limit the output of legislation and bias it the direction of serving the public good.

GOVERNMENT STRUCTURE

Take another look at the Constitution, and behold its formal structure: Article I, the legislative power;

Article II, the executive power; and Article III, the judicial power. The powers are *functionally separated*: why?

One reason is specialization. We want our laws to be carefully considered and, moreover, to be tolerably fair compromises among varying interests. This objective requires a legislative body that is numerous, broadly reflective of society, and deliberative. But we also want government to act promptly (for example, in response to emergencies or attacks); that objective requires a single executive who can act with "energy and dispatch," as *The Federalist* puts it. We want laws to be impartially applied, which requires judges operating at a remove from politics and electoral pressures.

There is a second reason for the separation of powers: the combination of all those powers in a single body is "the very definition of tyranny" (*Federalist* 47). A monopoly of power is dangerous; hence, you separate the institutions.

However, doing so in writing—on "parchment"— is not enough: one has to ensure that the institutional actors follow the rules. The answer to this difficulty is what modern theorists call "self-enforcing" rules and the founders called "checks and balances." The idea is to make officials' selfish motivations work *for* citizens, not against them: rival institutions can be made to check one another. To that end, the occupants of the various branches of government must be given "the necessary constitutional means, and personal motives, to resist encroachment of the others.... Ambition must be made to counteract ambition" (*Federalist* 51).

The principal means of endowing officeholders with rival motives is to make the institutions answer to different constituencies or rather to differently composed constituencies. Your representative, your senator, and your president all represent you. But none can claim to do so unambiguously or exclusively. The point of the design is to make sovereignty *contestable*. A constitution cannot prevent politicians from posturing as tribunes of the people. However, it can give politicians an incentive to contest their rivals' claims and to check their ambitions. Conflicts of this sort also remind us that for constitutional purposes, there is only one sovereign in America: *we*. The various government institutions are merely our agents. (*Federalist* 45 contains Madison's most forceful statement of this argument.)

To make the system work, one must give institutions the means to resist one another. "Checks and balances" require some mixing of legislative, executive, and judicial functions, rather than a rigid and complete separation. Foremost, the Constitution contains a system of veto rights:

no law can go into effect (or remain in effect) without the assent of all branches of government.[3] By establishing institutional competition, then, the Constitution compels cooperation. The expectation is that cooperation will occur only on terms that are broadly acceptable, because they have been thoroughly vetted by rival, competing institutions.

Note how closely this constitutional design is tied to the Constitution's other principles, especially minimalism and decision rules: you (citizen) can trust competitive politics because we (the founders) got the institutional rules right. You will not like the results in this, that, or the other particular case, including cases you may feel very strongly about. However, the results will remain within reasonable bounds.

---

[3] Note how carefully the Constitution is written to reflect both the separation of powers and their mixing and mutual checking. Although the veto is exercised by the chief executive, it is contained in Article I §7: it is a legislative power. Conversely, the requirement that the Senate (a legislative branch) must provide "advice and consent" to presidential appointments is listed in Article II §2 because appointment is an executive power. At the same time, the Constitution explicitly "vests" legislative (Article I), executive (Article II), and judicial (Article III) power in the Congress, president, and federal courts, respectively. Combining or transferring those powers is prohibited unless the Constitution explicitly provides for it.

HAS IT WORKED?

The Constitution's competitive arrangements are expected to do double duty: they must ensure broadly acceptable policy outcomes, and they must protect the institutions themselves over time. In some respects, the ingenious design seems to have performed admirably. Political scientists have at various times written and complained about an "Imperial Presidency" (especially during and after armed conflicts), an "Imperial Congress," even an "Imperial Court." However, the empires have waxed and waned. Experience suggests that the constitutional system has potent self-correcting mechanisms. Ambition continues to counteract ambition. But the picture also has a dark side.

The central problem with the Madisonian design is not that institutional actors may drop their guard; it is that they may *collude* to expand their power, jointly and severally. Madison's premise is that the people's agents may all too easily betray their constituents and, so to speak, go into business for themselves. Because it is very difficult for citizens to monitor their agents' behavior, we need "auxiliary precautions" and institutional competition. The theory implies, however, that all officeholders have a common problem: voters and taxpayers will insist on holding them responsible. Thus, despite their rivalries, institutional actors have a common interest in creating arrangements that make the citizens' monitoring job more difficult.

Two very large sets of modern institutional arrangements can be understood as products of such intergovernmental collusion. One of them, discussed in chapter 9, is the administrative state, composed of agencies that combine legislative, executive, and judicial functions under a single organizational umbrella. The other is the oldest question of American law: federalism.

5

FEDERALISM

The United States Constitution contains three major institutional innovations: the separation of powers, judicial review of legislative enactments, and federalism. Among these, federalism—in the form of the Constitution—is the most accidental invention. And to this day, it is the most misunderstood invention. Federalism often serves as a synonym for decentralization, and it is usually discussed as a question of "balance" and degree: how much power should states retain against, or relative to, the national government? The obsession with this question dates back all the way to the founding of the country. However, this is the wrong question, and the Constitution provides no answer (see box 3). The founders' problem, to which the Constitution does provide an answer, is *what kind* of federalism we should have.

Box 3: What Is Federalism?
Many federal systems (for example, India's, Germany's, and the European Union's) strive for a balance between levels of government. Their constitutions all contain some equilibrating or balancing rule, as well as formal mechanisms

(for example, revenue transfers) to maintain or adjust the balance.

The omission of any such rule in the United States Constitution is both conspicuous and deliberate. The Tenth Amendment has often been read as a state-protective balancing rule, but the text lends little support to that interpretation: the amendment merely says that the federal government shall have the powers that it has. The allocation of powers is the constitutional baseline regardless of its effects on the federal-state "balance" over time.

CONSTITUTIONAL FORMS

Under the Articles of Confederation, the states formed a federal union, not unlike the contemporary European Union. However, the Articles did not permit the Congress—then an assembly of states—to govern and tax citizens. Instead, states had to agree unanimously to collect and contribute taxes to the union. During the Revolutionary War, states had repeatedly failed to remit agreed-upon contributions ("requisitions"), greatly imperiling the union's overstretched army. After the war, the system left states and the union with crushing debts and no practical way to pay them. To remedy the situation, Alexander Hamilton urged in *Federalist* 15 that the union had to be cured of its central defect: the national government had to have authority to tax and regulate citizens *directly*, without reliance on the states.

Once you admit Hamilton's point, it follows that the central government must be elected by and be accountable to those whom it governs—citizens, not states. However, once you have a central representative government that governs directly, what good are the states?[4] Not a lot, Hamilton and even Madison thought: at the Philadelphia Convention, they urged that the states should be effectively abolished (although they could be "subordinately useful" as administrative subunits of the national government). That proposal, though, was bound to fail: the thirteen states existed with their own institutions, interests, and political traditions. If there was to be a union at all, some form of federalism was a foregone conclusion. The

---

[4] The question becomes especially urgent in light of the argument of *Federalist* 10 (discussed earlier): if states are playpens of "factions" and the national government will behave better, why have states?

founders' ingenious response to this difficulty was to *limit* and *enumerate* the national government's powers, while leaving all else to the states.

This is what James Madison called the "compound republic." The federal government's powers, he writes in *Federalist* 39, are "national" in their *operation*: they operate directly on citizens, and every federal law trumps any state law. (This is the meaning of the supremacy clause, Article VI §2.) The powers are "federal" in their *extent* because they are enumerated and limited, generally to matters of national concern: defense and foreign relations; national and foreign commerce; patents and post roads. All else is left to the states. Because the federal government and the states occupy different "spheres," this constitutional arrangement is often called "dual federalism."

FROM "DUAL" TO "COOPERATIVE" FEDERALISM

From the outset, federal-state relations proved extremely contentious and often unstable. Over the centuries, Madison's "compound republic" has undergone momentous changes. One set of changes, discussed in later chapters, has to do with the Civil War and the amendments enacted in its wake. Another set has to do with institutional responses to the dramatic economic, social, and political changes of the early twentieth century. Industrialization and economic integration, especially the emergence of gigantic private corporations, prompted urgent social demands for government regulation. Congress began to regulate matters that once had been deemed beyond its powers, such as labor conditions and agricultural production. At the same time, states regulated interstate commerce and its principal actors (corporations) much more aggressively. Thus, once-distinct federal and state powers came to run over one and the same "sphere," encompassing virtually any private activity in the country.

That reality, in turn, required increased coordination between federal and state actors. It is still the case that Congress may not govern (or, as the Supreme Court says, "commandeer") the states. However, Congress may *pay* state and local governments to do its bidding, and the junior governments may freely accept such offers. Beginning (roughly) after World War I, the national government adopted small grant programs to build roads and to assist indigent mothers. With President Franklin Delano Roosevelt's New Deal in the 1930s and the social program of the Great Society in the 1960s, federally funded but state-implemented "conditional grants" programs came to cover a vast array of policies, including education, the environment, welfare, health care (especially Medicaid), infrastructure, and, most recently, homeland security and immigration. The dual federalism of the compound republic has given way to "cooperative federalism."

What explains federalism's wholesale transformation? Many social scientists view it as an inevitable adjustment to a complex, interconnected economy and society. Much can be said for this interpretation, but it is a bit too facile. The founders were perfectly attuned to economic complexity and well aware of the forces of economic innovation and integration. Still, they deemed it possible to maintain some sensible division of power between the levels of government. What (if anything) went wrong?

Federalism's transformation makes sense in light of the constitutional principle described in chapter 4: competition. The Constitution forbids states to interfere with interstate commerce, and it allows citizens to choose their own state—where to live and where to do business. (Can you identify some of the specific constitutional provisions?) If a state overtaxes or overregulates productive citizens, those citizens will move to (or do business in) a more hospitable state. Retirees move to Florida because it has no income tax; retail businesses often locate in states without a sales tax. In a highly mobile country, competition for productive citizens powerfully constrains what any local government can demand from or impose on its citizens.

State governments loathe the competition. Contrary to a widespread but erroneous belief, therefore, state politicians (as a class) do not want a limited federal government. Rather, they want an unlimited central government that stands ready to eradicate competition. A federal minimum wage, for example, protects high-wage states against competition from lower-wage states. Similarly, competition will often constrain states' ability to tax. Their governments will often be better off if the federal government first taxes on a national basis and then sends money back to the states, even if the money comes with some conditions. Such arrangements, as just noted, are the hallmark of "cooperative" federalism. Economists call them "cartels," meaning agreements among rivals to limit or eliminate competition.

Against this backdrop, the transition from dual to cooperative federalism boils down to a question: what prevented states in the nineteenth century from creating federally sponsored cartels and allowed them to do so thereafter? The best answer is the deep divide among states, first over slavery and then over segregation and the so-called Jim Crow laws. That divide prevented states from agreeing on federal regulatory and spending programs: terms that would have been acceptable to the South were unacceptable to the North, and vice versa. Only the harrowing economic crisis and the unusual political consensus of the New Deal produced conditions under which states could lock themselves into anticompetitive cartels, stabilized by federal minimum regulatory standards and massive federal-to-state transfer payments.

Needless to say, no one laments the demise of slavery and Jim Crow. Many federalism scholars, however, argue that cooperative federalism has unfortunate consequences—tendencies to obscure political accountability and to induce excessive spending at all levels of government. Box 4 provides illustrations.

Box 4: Cooperative Federalism's Discontents
K–12 education is jointly funded and regulated by the federal, state, and local governments. The federal government supplies approximately 10 percent of K–12 funding. In return for those dollars, should it exercise greater or lesser control over local schools (say, teacher qualifications

or curricula)? When local schools fail, whose responsibility is that—and whom would you hold accountable?

Under the federal Medicaid statute, the federal government reimburses between roughly 50 and 80 cents of every dollar states spend on medical services for some (not all) poor citizens. The Affordable Care Act ("Obamacare" to its opponents) presented states with a choice: either you agree to expand Medicaid (on more favorable funding conditions), or else *all* your Medicaid funding may be withheld. In a 7–2 decision in *NFIB* v. *Sebelius* (2012), the Supreme Court held that this supposedly "cooperative" scheme amounted to unconstitutional "coercion" of state governments. Do you agree? If the federal government pays the piper, why can't it call the tune?

In thinking about the answer, consider that when the federal government pays fifty cents of every dollar a state spends on Medicaid, the service will look much cheaper to the local taxpayers than it actually is. The taxpayers will ignore or forget that they are also paying for the subsidy through their federal income tax (economists call this a "fiscal illusion"). Moreover, even if a state were to withdraw from the program altogether, its citizens would still pay for the federal share: the money would simply flow to other states. Thus, all states have a powerful incentive to maximize "their" share of the program, and none can withdraw. Should we call this "coercion"—and what exactly is problematic about it?

All else equal, cooperative funding programs will grow much faster than programs funded by a single (state or federal) government. Can you explain why? Is that an argument for or against such programs?

6

CONSTITUTIONAL RIGHTS AND STRUCTURE

So far, we have examined the Constitution's structure. I have postponed a discussion of constitutional rights, not because our rights to freedom of speech, a jury trial, and due process are unimportant (they are very important) but rather to track the founders' theory: the constitutional structure comes first. Rights must be understood within that larger competitive structure.

Modern sensibilities run up hard against that approach. Rights, we tend to think, are far more fundamental—and are certainly easier to understand—than questions of government organization. However, much can be said for the founders' more hard-nosed view. Even dictators know how to create a bill of rights: witness the Soviet and Chinese constitutions. For protecting freedom, we may find it more useful to think in terms of limiting government powers than in terms of long lists of rights. Hamilton had that in mind in calling the Constitution "to every useful purpose, a BILL OF RIGHTS" (*Federalist* 84).

This, though, is not quite the end of the matter. While one can imagine a constitution that is all structure and no rights, the United States Constitution embodies a different strategy. The unamended text itself contains guarantees of individual rights (can you list them?), and the soon-ratified Bill of Rights added many others. The rights, however, are carefully calculated to reinforce the constitutional structure and to operate in harmony with it. In the apt phrase of Yale Law School professor Akhil Amar, we should (with Hamilton) understand the Constitution as a Bill of Rights—and the "Bill of Rights as a Constitution." The text and structure of the Bill of Rights provide compelling reasons to understand rights in harmony and continuity with the structure.[5]

RIGHTS: FORMAL PRINCIPLES

Recall some of the Constitution's structural principles: minimalism; decision rules, not distributions; and competition. The same formal principles run through the Bill of Rights.

As for minimalism, the Constitution's rights inventory is quite limited, especially in comparison with modern, rights-rich constitutions. And note this striking fact: while we tend to think of rights as sacrosanct realms of private autonomy beyond

---

[5] So does history. James Madison, who shepherded the amendments that would become the Bill of Rights through the First Congress, took great care to block proposals that ranked atop the Antifederalists' agenda— prominently, to limit federal tax powers and standing armies. Those proposals would have undermined the Constitution's carefully wrought structure. The twelve amendments that were submitted for ratification, including the ten that made it into the Constitution, did not.

the reach of government, the text of the Bill of Rights suggests a very different understanding. For example, under the Fifth Amendment, any private property, and indeed all of it, may be taken for public use, provided just compensation is paid; and life, liberty, and property may be taken, so long as due process is observed. With the arguable exception of the First Amendment, no private conduct seems entirely immune to public regulation. With rights as with government powers, the constitutional architecture reflects a bold confidence that we can leave a lot to politics.

Next, just as the Constitution contains no structural principles of distribution, it contains no distributional rights. Box 5 provides examples of welfare rights contained in other nations' constitutions. Our constitution contains nothing of

---

[6] Our rights are also nondistributional in another, subtler sense: they do not permit a weighing of social costs and benefits. Rights are limited prohibitions against specified forms of government conduct; but where and when they hold, they really hold: the government may not escape the prohibitions even if it finds a weighty reason for doing so. For example, it may seem gratuitous or even cruel to allow rapists or child molesters to confront their accusers in court, but we do not allow prosecutors, judges, or legislators to weigh the costs and benefits of confrontation. The confrontation clause of the Sixth Amendment has made that decision for us.

the kind, and the Supreme Court has consistently rejected attempts to read such rights into the document.[6]

Box 5: Constitutional Welfare Rights

ART. 27, CONSTITUTION OF THE REPUBLIC OF SOUTH AFRICA (1996)

Everyone has the right to have access to-

a. health care services, including reproductive health care;

b. sufficient food and water; and

c. social security, including, if they are unable to support themselves and their dependents, appropriate social assistance.

ART. 45, CONSTITUTION OF THE PEOPLE'S REPUBLIC OF CHINA (1982)

Citizens of the People's Republic of China have the right to material assistance from the State and society when they are old, ill or disabled. The State develops social insurance, social relief and medical and health services that are required for citizens to enjoy this right.

ART. 14BIS, CONSTITUTION OF ARGENTINA (1957)
The State shall grant the benefits of social security, which shall be of an integral nature and may not be waived. In particular, the laws shall establish: compulsory social...insurance, which shall be in charge of national or provincial entities with financial and economic autonomy, administered by the interested parties with State participation, with no overlapping of contributions; adjustable retirements and pensions; full family protection; protection of homestead; family allowances and access to a worthy housing.

Finally, rights conform to the constitutional principle of institutional competition. As a rule, rights guarantees run not against "the State" or "the government" at large but against particular institutions—sometimes in so many words, sometimes by clear implication. The clearest and most common line of distinction and differentiation runs between the states and national institutions. For example, the prohibition against impairments of the obligation of contract (Art. I §10) applies only against the states (and apparently only their legislatures, not their courts); the provisions of the Bill of Rights, in their original understanding, apply only against federal institutions. The principle of competition provides a way to understand this arrangement. At the state level, state competition allows citizens to migrate from an oppressive state to a more rights-protective state.[7] The national government, in contrast, is a monopolist: we cannot run from it without leaving the country. Where competition fails, we need rights (see box 6).

Box 6: Rights, Religion, and Competition

The First Amendment provides a splendid illustration of the interplay between the Bill of Rights and the competitive constitutional structure. The amendment forbids, among other things, any (federal) law "respecting an establishment of religion." While the precise meaning of this establishment clause

---

[7] As discussed below, the protection is imperfect, but it is no mere theory. The dynamic has played a powerful role in American history—for example, in the northward migration of African-Americans from oppressive Southern states.

is controversial, the provision is clearly procompetitive in at least one and, depending on how you interpret the clause, probably two respects.

The first, unambiguously procompetitive effect stems from the separation of church and state that the establishment clause requires. The clause quite clearly forbids an arrangement such as Germany's, in which churches are supported from income tax surcharges on taxpayers who declare themselves members of a particular faith. Germany's model is entirely consistent with the free exercise of religion, equal protection, and government neutrality: no one is compelled to pay the surcharge, and the proceeds of the tax are distributed to religious denominations in proportion to membership. The principal difference is that Germany's system is not competitive. Ours is: if churches, synagogues, or mosques wish to survive and thrive, they will have to do so without the government's assistance and in competition with rival denominations.

The second, more contestable competitive effect of the establishment clause has to do with federalism. By its words and in its original understanding, the clause forbids Congress but not the states to enact laws "respecting" establishment. Thus, states could, and in the early decades of the republic did, establish official state churches and religions. States, you could say, "competed" for members of particular denominations, and they offered different models of church-state relations.

In the modern era, the establishment clause was "incorporated" and made applicable to the states along with virtually the entire Bill of Rights. However, prominent scholars and justices continue to argue that the establishment clause "resists" incorporation, principally for the (competitive) federalism reason just stated.

RIGHTS AND STRUCTURE: EXAMPLES AND DIFFICULTIES

A few examples help illustrate the ways in which rights align with the constitutional structure, as well as the difficulties that arise under the scheme.

Some rights serve as structure-protective *enforcement* mechanisms. For example, the privileges and immunities clause (Article IV §2) entitles "the Citizens of each State ... to all Privileges and

Immunities of Citizens in the several States." This clause means that states must not discriminate against outsiders: if state citizens may conduct this or that business without hindrance, the state must allow noncitizens to do likewise. To be sure, Congress could prohibit state interferences under its enumerated powers. However, the founders feared that Congress would often fail to do so. The privileges and immunities clause—a grant of right—enables private citizens to enforce the federal structure and its competitive protections in federal court.

Other rights are *continuous* with the constitutional structure. Ordinarily (the argument runs), the checks and balances of a competitive constitutional structure will provide adequate protection. However, that calculus does not apply when particular individuals have already been singled out for special adverse treatment. This concern helps explain the prominence of criminal process protections in the Bill of Rights: they cover situations in which a lone individual finds himself confronted with the combined might of the community. The Fifth Amendment protection against uncompensated "takings" of private property rests on the same logic.

The greatest difficulties in matching rights with structure arise in connection with the Constitution's *federal* structure. As just noted, the Bill of Rights was initially understood to apply only against federal institutions, not against the states. That understanding changed with the enactment of the Fourteenth Amendment, discussed in chapter 8; the remarks here concern the general constitutional rationale.

Although state competition, as noted, often provides powerful protection against government abuse, that is not the case when the cost of leaving an oppressive state becomes prohibitive. For example, local governments cannot easily exploit a software business, which can operate just about anywhere. But they *can* exploit a local small business (say, a bakery) that cannot transport its customer base and accumulated goodwill into another jurisdiction. Or states may "overregulate" abortion (and, in an earlier age, contraceptives) because the move across state lines is too expensive for many local citizens. Gay ecologists may find that no state provides a right to marriage *and* a high-mountain environment.

Should we tolerate such abuses (or inefficiencies, depending on your view)—or block them by means of universal rights, even at some cost to democracy and state competition? An enormous swath of the Supreme Court's rights jurisprudence can be understood in light of this dilemma. In the decades preceding the New Deal, the Court protected economic rights under a theory of "substantive due process." The most famous of these cases was *Lochner* v. *New York* (1905), in which the Court held that a state law limiting working hours in bakeries violated the Constitution. After the New Deal, *Lochner*-type "economic" rights became anathema, but the Supreme Court protected "personal" rights on a very similar theory. The abortion decision in *Roe* v. *Wade* (1973) is the most famous and consequential of these cases.

The next chapter will revisit the rights question. The point to remember is that there is no tidy solution to the trade-off between universal rights on the one hand and democracy and competition on the other. Expansive rights will grant more power to the Court and leave less room for democratic politics. That sounds unattractive; but then, it is also hard to say anything very nice about local politics that produce a "grassroots tyranny." We have to pick our institutional poison.

7

JUDICIAL REVIEW

The tensions and the delicate interplay between constitutional rights and constitutional structure are reflected in the United States Supreme Court's decisions and its role in the constitutional system. We have come to associate the Court almost exclusively with the protection of individual rights—to racial equality, free speech, and much else. That view, however, is much too simple. Remember the Supreme Court's controversial 2012 decision over "Obamacare"? You could say that the case arose over citizens' "right" not to be compelled to purchase health insurance. Fundamentally, however, the case was about the federal government's power to enact the statute in the first place, and no individual rights provision was at issue in the case. In short, the case was principally about the constitutional structure. It helps to think about the Supreme Court and its institutional role—including its rights-protective function—in that broader and now-familiar context.

COORDINATION

A written constitution, designed for many generations, must be rigid, yet adaptable—both because the drafters, being human, may make mistakes and because later generations may decide in light of experience, changed circumstances, and democratic deliberation that this or that aspect of the constitutional design requires reform. The primary means of ensuring stability (as opposed to either sclerosis or constant upheaval), we have seen, is institutional competition. However, that answer is not quite enough, because institutional actors may come to disagree over what the rules of the constitutional game are. The president needs the Senate's advice and consent to appoint a secretary of state; may he *remove* her on his own authority? May Congress establish a bank of the United States? The constitutional text provides no definitive answers to these and many similar questions.

Intergovernmental conflicts arise with particular frequency in federal systems such as ours. If Congress may establish a bank, may states tax it? May Congress prohibit the cultivation of marijuana for private use, or does the Constitution leave such matters to the states? Again, the Constitution does not directly answer many conflicts and questions of this sort.[8] Lest unresolved conflict grind the enterprise to a halt, some third party must supply an answer.

---

[8] The questions about the bank arose in the famous case of *M'Culloch v. Maryland* (1819)—arguably Chief Justice John Marshall's greatest opinion and by any measure one of the most important cases in our history. The marijuana question was asked and answered in *Gonzales v. Raich* (2005). You will find the cases in any textbook on constitutional law.

One possible arbiter is the electorate. Thomas Jefferson was a prominent advocate of submitting conflicts among the branches directly to a popular vote. However, the founders firmly rejected his proposal, arguing that it would likely inflame public passions and undermine constitutional stability. The Constitution leaves the door open to amendments; and over the centuries, many amendments have served to "fix" institutional problems, from presidential elections (the Twelfth Amendment) to the District of Columbia (the Twenty-Third Amendment). As we have seen, however, the amendment process is arduous and not intended as a routine recourse to the people.

Another possible solution, especially with respect to conflicts between states and the national government, is to leave questions of constitutionality to the states. In the decades after the founding, that position—often called "interposition" or "nullification"—played a large role, especially in controversies over the federal Alien and Sedition Acts and, later, the national tariff. However (and to make a complicated story very short), the Constitution provides no ground for the theory, for good reason: if states were to disagree among themselves, the conflicts would remain unresolved— or the country could come apart. The Civil War settled the nullification question once and for all.

That leaves only one other option: an independent court with the power "to say what the law is," as the great Chief Justice John Marshall put it. To be effective, that power must encompass the power to declare that another branch of government has violated the law, which in turn includes the power to declare that the branch that makes the law, the Congress, has transgressed the one federal law that it has not made and cannot make—the Constitution. This power of judicial review—that is, the power to declare acts of Congress unconstitutional—is not explicitly granted in the Constitution. However, it is quite plainly implied by a *written* constitution. Conflicts will arise between the constitutional text and the will of a temporary popular and legislative majority. It seems odd to entrust the resolution of such conflicts to those majorities and far more compelling to commit it to an independent court. John Marshall's decision and opinion in *Marbury* v. *Madison* (1803) firmly enshrined judicial review in our constitutional law. (You should read the case or at least a summary: it is the most famous decision by any court, ever.)

INSTITUTIONAL DESIGN

Marbury's theory has become almost universally accepted; in fact, it was already fairly conventional at the time. However, it is not entirely free from doubt. While the Constitution cannot mean whatever Congress says it means, it seems equally implausible to insist (at least in a democracy) that it means whatever five out of nine Supreme Court justices say it means. There has to be some way to reconcile the rival claims of constitutional legality and democracy.

One plausible institutional response, adopted in varying forms by many countries, is to create a specialized constitutional court and to keep it close to the political branches. For example, the legislature may consult the constitutional court's expert opinion on pending legislation before it is enacted, which greatly reduces the prospect that the judiciary will "strike down" a democratically enacted law.

The U.S. Supreme Court, in contrast, is *not* a specialized constitutional court. Under Article III of the Constitution, its jurisdiction—meaning "the power to say what the law is"—extends to many kinds of cases. Instead, the Court's power to adjudicate constitutional questions stems from the fact that it is a *court* authorized under Article III to hear legal "cases and controversies" arising under, among other legal sources, the Constitution. When a legal case within its jurisdiction happens to present a conflict between a (federal) law and the Constitution, the Court cannot decline to act as a court: its unpleasant duty is to declare the law invalid. However, the Court's power of judicial review remains limited by its "court-ness": that is, if the case does not fall within the Court's jurisdiction, the Court has no power to provide judicial review.

Some implications of this arrangement may strike you as bizarre. On the one hand, the Supreme Court will hear divorce or inheritance cases within its jurisdiction. On the other hand, the power of judicial review belongs to the entire federal judiciary—not just the Supreme Court but also lower courts. (Even district courts have exercised the authority, although not very frequently.) Trivial disputes may occasion grand constitutional rulings, while pesky conflicts among political institutions may go unaddressed simply because no plaintiff with a legal case will come forward.

We live with these oddities because they are the price of more highly valued objectives. Constitutionalism demands a difference between the higher law of the Constitution and democratic politics. Maintaining that difference, in turn, demands a distance between the political branches and the courts. *Democratic* constitutionalism means that the Court must not be a disembodied "guardian of the Constitution" that hovers above our politics. Democratic *constitutionalism* demands that the Court act as an independent, competitive check on the process, not as a governmental co-conspirator.

RIGHTS REVISITED

Judicial review, in the form just sketched, is closely tied to the constitutional structure and the need for institutional coordination. Nowadays, in contrast, big Supreme Court cases more commonly arise over constitutional rights. This shift from structure to rights in the Court's emphasis dates back to the era of the New Deal in the 1930s. In the wake of the Great Depression, governments at all levels (local, state, and federal) demanded far greater authority to intervene in the economy than the Supreme Court's doctrines—a "Constitution for the horse and buggy era," President Franklin Delano Roosevelt called it—seemed to permit. Eventually, the Court abandoned many of the structural limitations that, under its earlier understanding, barred democratic majorities from having their way. For example, the Court greatly expanded the authority of both Congress and states to regulate commerce. As the system became more democratic, however, it also became more troublesome to constituencies that tend to lose in a political free-for-all. Thus, having weakened the Constitution's competitive political structure, the Court gravitated toward a jurisprudence that revolves around the rights of individuals or minorities.[9]

The shift may have been inevitable, but it entails a more difficult problem and a harsher debate than those of a more structure-oriented judicial review. It is easy to see why a democratic country would want the ground rules of competitive politics policed by a third party; it is much harder to see why it would subject the results of that process to review by an unelected elite. While the question may have plausible answers, rights review does increase the tension between politics and law, democracy and courts. You can see that conflict in every Supreme Court case over contested moral issues and in the increasingly acrimonious fights over judicial appointments.

---

[9] The most widely accepted statement of this new orientation is a famous footnote (footnote 4) in a case called *Carolene Products Co. v. United States* (1938).

8

**SLAVERY AND THE
SECOND FOUNDING**

Over America's heroic founding and the Constitution hangs the large, grim shadow of slavery. Naturally, we are preoccupied with slavery's moral dimensions: its sheer inhumanity, its jarring conflict with the ideals of the Declaration of Independence, the toll that it would take to eradicate the institution, and the sorrowful legacy it would leave for American society for many more decades. On top of all that, though, the slavery question produced a bargain that was fundamentally at odds with the constitutional principles of America's founding.

The Constitution carefully avoids any direct mention of slavery. However, it contains—or rather contained, prior to the Civil War Amendments— institutional arrangements that reflect an uneasy, dreadful compromise on the issue. Foremost, it apportioned seats in the House of Representatives, as well as direct taxation, in accordance with each state's population, "which shall be determined by adding to the whole Number of free Persons ... three fifths of all other Persons"—that is, slaves (Article I, §2 Cl. 3). This compromise allowed the Constitutional Convention to negotiate the deep divide over slavery. The South gained disproportionate representation in the House of Representatives and the Electoral College (which elects the president), helping it protect its peculiar institution for many decades. For the North, the bargain held the promise that the South might be taxed for the privilege.

It is difficult to imagine an arrangement more radically at odds with the Constitution's general thrust and structure. The formula is distributive and was calculated to "freeze" a preconceived balance among political and economic forces. Not only is that bargain sordid; measured by the founders' own theory of "reflection and choice," it is not even constitutional. However, the problem has an additional dimension.

Popular sovereignty and equality under the law are empty concepts unless you specify who counts as a person and a citizen. No genuine political union can leave that question to its member-states: the principle that no state may deprive citizens of the United States of their elementary rights follows directly from the nature of a federal constitution as the constitutive act of a single, sovereign people. The founders punted on that point not because they failed to see it but because they thought that evasion was the tragic but necessary price of union. That judgment may have been right, but it left their constitutional project in need of completion.

THE CIVIL WAR AMENDMENTS

The Civil War and the constitutional amendments ratified in its wake belatedly undid the Constitutional

Convention's slavery bargain. However, that is not all that they did. Both slavery and the three-fifth formula were erased by the Thirteenth Amendment. The Fourteenth and Fifteenth Amendments remedied the Constitution's deeper design flaws. First, the Fourteenth Amendment clarified as a matter of federal law *who counts* as a person and a citizen. Second, the amendments empowered Congress to enforce the constitutional requirements "by appropriate legislation." Third, the Fourteenth Amendment established or extended rights against the states: due process, equal protection, and the "privileges or immunities of citizens of the United States."

In the first two respects, the Civil War Amendments are unequivocally compatible with the structure of the Constitution and serve to complete it. Harder questions arise over the extension of constitutional rights vis-à-vis the states.

SYNTHESIS

Surprisingly, the Supreme Court's first major engagement with the Fourteenth Amendment had nothing to do with race or the legacy of slavery. In the *Slaughter-House Cases* (1872), Louisiana citizens complained that a local law, granting several slaughterhouses a monopoly over the trade, violated the new Fourteenth Amendment protection against state infringements of "privileges or immunities" (here, the asserted privilege of engaging in lawful commerce). A sharply divided Supreme Court held that the privileges or immunities clause protects only the rights held by individuals as United States citizens, which—in the Court's reading— seemed to include little beyond moving about the country. Most legal scholars and historians now believe this interpretation to be mistaken. The "privileges or immunities" guaranteed by the Fourteenth Amendment, they say, plainly include the protections of the Bill of Rights. Other scholars defend the Court's rejection of an expansive interpretation that would prompt the routine invalidation of local health and safety regulations. That consequence, they say, is far removed from the concerns that prompted the amendment and would leave far too little of federalism.

No such controversy, in contrast, surrounds the Supreme Court's subsequent shameful failures to enforce the Civil War Amendments in direct confrontations with the Southern social structure. In *United States v. Cruikshank* (1875), the justices refused to make a federal judicial forum available to black citizens where the local courts could not possibly be trusted. And in the notorious *Plessy v. Ferguson* decision (1896), the origin of the "separate but equal doctrine," the Court upheld a state law requiring racial segregation of passengers. That holding failed to protect interstate carriers, which had enjoyed protection against exploitative state regulation even before the Civil War Amendments, against segregationist state laws. The completion of the constitutional project would take a full half-century, when the civil rights revolution, beginning with the Supreme Court's famous decision in *Brown v. Board of Education* (1954), made good on the promise of equal citizenship.[10]

The equally painful and inspiring progress of civil rights powerfully illustrates that no constitution implements itself. Nor does history readily follow judicial edicts. Most historians agree that it was not so much the landmark decision in *Brown v. Board* but the civil rights legislation of the 1960s that finally broke the back of state-imposed segregation in the South. Constitutional government is always a work of construction—not just in a law professor's study or a judge's chambers (although that is part of it), but in public debate, institutional politics, and the projection of public authority.

---

[10] At roughly the same time, the Supreme Court "incorporated" the Bill of Rights into the Fourteenth Amendment (under the due process clause, not the privileges or immunities clause), thus making the rights enforceable against the states.

9

THE ADMINISTRATIVE STATE

Congress makes laws, subject to presidential presentment and veto. The executive enforces the law. In cases of overreach, courts will provide redress. Or so we learned in grade school. In real life, in contrast, few of the rules of public law that govern us come from Congress, or for that matter, state legislatures. The vast bulk comes from special-purpose agencies—the Federal Trade Commission, the Securities Exchange Commission, the Environmental Protection Agency, and so on through the alphabet. These agencies regulate financial markets, the media, workplaces, health insurance, pensions, and products from cars to pharmaceuticals, from lawn darts to Buckyballs. (If you don't recognize those products, that's because the Consumer Products Safety Commission has effectively banned their sale.)

We often chafe at the bureaucracy, and we are not alone: public grumbling over "faceless bureaucrats" is common in all developed democracies. Only in the United States, however, has public administration been a perennial *constitutional* problem.

In France and Germany, bureaucracies are governed by a rigid body of "administrative law." Centuries of legal thought, long predating the arrival of liberal-democratic constitutions in those countries, have gone into its formulation, and the system has withstood profound social and

> "We often chafe at the bureaucracy, and we
> are not alone: public grumbling over 'faceless
> bureaucrats' is common in all developed
> democracies. Only in the United States, however,
> has public administration been a perennial
> constitutional problem."

even constitutional changes. In the United States, in contrast, administrative law emerged only at the beginning of the twentieth century, in fits and starts and in an improvisational interplay between the Congress and the Supreme Court. In over a full century, we have never quite figured out what to do with or about the administrative state. Why?

BUREAUCRACY AND THE CONSTITUTION
The Constitution plainly envisions some bureaucracies. Standing armies must be raised and equipped; tariffs must be administered; taxes must be assessed and collected; patents must be registered; the mail must be delivered; a census must be taken every ten years. In a very large country,

those tasks will require swarms of officers, and their
organization posed both practical and political
problems throughout the nineteenth century.[II]
None of this, however, posed any great *constitutional*
problem. Agencies were either subject to direct
political control (as with the War Department,
now called the Department of Defense), or else
their functions were routine and ministerial. Your
mailman may be late on occasion, but he is not a
menace to the Constitution.

The "administration" that does pose
constitutional difficulties is the combination of
executive, judicial, and legislative powers within
agencies that are insulated from direct executive
control—most commonly, through legislative
provisions that bar the president from removing the
agencies' officers. Our three-branch, separation-
of-powers Constitution resists an independent
"fourth branch" that combines all powers. Why have
we nonetheless entrusted so much power to that
pseudo-branch?

[II] Some of those problems and their solutions now strike us as quite
comical. The first federal patent statute, for example, provided that
patents had to be approved by the (then, three) members of the
cabinet. For obvious reasons, that arrangement did not last very long.

The common answer hangs on the needs of a complex, advanced society (see box 7). Such a society, the argument runs, demands a great deal of *expertise*—more expertise than even a very well-staffed legislature (such as the Congress) can manage.

Box 7: Origins of the Administrative State

A complex society will have to run some industries—railroads, telegraphs, telephones, electricity—as public utilities. Throughout our history, however, we have shied away from simply nationalizing private enterprises. Instead, we run them as regulated industries that, technically, remain private. That status, in turn, entails a doctrine, derived from the due process clause and in effect to this day, that the utilities must be allowed to earn a reasonable rate of return. What is that rate, and who should determine it? Congress cannot possibly know what the rates should be for any given utility in a vast and diverse country. The Supreme Court might be able to invalidate egregious regulations, but it is not designed to review thousands of rate-making decisions continually. Considerations of this sort prompted the creation of the first "independent" agency, the Interstate Commerce Commission, in 1887.

The need seems compelling, but then so do the doubts that are bound to arise in a constitutional culture that prizes democratic accountability and lawful government. Proposals to bring the "headless fourth branch" under constitutional control have accompanied the rise of the administrative state ever since its creation. Some critics insist on more specific instructions from Congress. *All* legislative power granted by the Constitution, they say, is vested in the Congress; it cannot be delegated willy-nilly to administrative agencies. Others propose to subordinate administrative agencies to the president's control, under a theory that is known as the "unitary executive." A third solution is to subject agencies to stringent judicial oversight. However, all those strategies conflict both with the demand for expertise and with one another.[12] If there is an elegant and efficient constitutional solution, it has yet to be found.

THE LIMITS OF ADMINISTRATION

The late James Q. Wilson, widely renowned as the greatest scholar of public administration over the past half-century, argued that conflicting objectives and dysfunctions afflict most public bureaucracies. The real problem, he argued, arises from inflated expectations of what government can realistically do. In the contemporary, media-driven world, problems quickly become crises; and when we have a crisis, government must act—regardless, it appears, of whether it can be expected to do much good.

The mismatch between government capacity and public expectations becomes particularly grave when we expect the *national* government to "do something" about the *local* conditions that affect us most directly, from crime to inadequate schools to workplace conditions and sexual harassment. Over the long distances and in the multiple channels through which federal money and directives must

---

[12] For example, in the interest of regularity and legality, we could subject food stamp eligibility determinations to full-scale due process requirements (short of jury trials). Considering the costs of administering such a system and the potential for error in hardship cases, we leave ample room for bureaucratic discretion—which also implies multiple errors, as well as a potential for fraud and abuse. Which is it to be?

travel, lots of things will go wrong, and the intended improvements may prove spotty or altogether elusive. At one level, we all understand this: witness the widespread resentment against "federal bureaucrats." At another level, we don't: no candidate for federal office proposes that Congress should do *nothing* about local problems.

Our ambivalence has a constitutional dimension. By deliberately fragmenting government power and authority, the Constitution offers multiple "opportunity points"—that is, channels for the discovery, articulation, and redress of citizens' grievances: some government agency, someplace, is always open for business. As we have seen, however, the Constitution also establishes "veto points" (checks and balances) to create a certain degree of government resistance to social demands—not because the demands are necessarily silly or frivolous but because constitutional government, being able to do only so much, should focus on tasks that it can reasonably hope to accomplish. The effect of the administrative state, as of "cooperative federalism," is to circumvent the veto points and to maximize the opportunity points. The rearrangement of the constitutional balance has a paradoxical effect: the more open government becomes to our entreaties, the more it seems to frustrate and disappoint us.

10

CONSTITUTIONAL CHANGE AND FIDELITY

The abolition of slavery, the Industrial Revolution, the administrative state, the New Deal and the Great Society, globalization, the Internet, and the information society: few of us would want to go back on any of those momentous social changes, and none of us can. And yet, we revert to the words and thoughts of long-dead founders who, for all their genius, had no clue about any of this. Why?

Part of the answer is that we are stuck with the Constitution. It may be imperfect, but its longevity is a considerable advantage. Lots of people can and do dream up a more perfect constitution. However, few would agree on what it should look like, and disagreements over basic questions of social organization are very time-consuming and costly to resolve. It is sensible to stick with known rules and arrangements, so long as they work tolerably well.

That response, though, prompts a further question: is there a way to remain faithful to the Constitution—across many generations, after enormous social changes, and amid the clatter and confusions of politics? Can we, should we, keep the Constitution in tune with the times—or should it be the other way around?

While the question may seem abstract, it plays a prominent role in our politics—in debates over judicial nominations to the Supreme Court, for example, and in raging controversies over Supreme

> *"Is there a way to remain faithful to the Constitution—across many generations, after enormous social changes, and amid the clatter and confusions of politics? Can we, should we, keep the Constitution in tune with the times— or should it be the other way around?"*

Court decisions. To oversimplify, one camp (of political liberals or "progressives") argues that the Constitution should be read to accommodate and perhaps to promote contemporary values and aspirations, from sexual autonomy to social equality. This position is often called "living" or "democratic" constitutionalism. The other, the conservative camp, insists that the Constitution must be read in its original meaning, as best we can determine it. This position is called "originalism."

Before concluding that one or the other side is ("obviously!") correct, you should view the debate in a broader constitutional and historical context. The Constitution itself creates the fidelity problem, anticipates it, and supplies some means of addressing it. That approach has a brilliant exponent in John Marshall, a leading member of the founding generation, and by nearly everyone's lights, the greatest Chief Justice of the United States Supreme Court.

JOHN MARSHALL'S CONSTITUTION

Because we are dealing with a written Constitution, our understanding must start with and remain anchored in the text. "It cannot be presumed," Marshall wrote in *Marbury* v. *Madison* (1803), "that any clause in the constitution is intended to be without effect." By that same token, you cannot make the words mean anything you want. Each word matters: why else was it written down?

However, the maxim that the words control is not quite enough for constitutional purposes. As Marshall observed in *M'Culloch* v. *Maryland* (1819), "we must never forget that it is a Constitution we are expounding," and a deliberately minimalist constitution at that. The Constitution differs from a zoning code or a mortgage lien in two respects: it is less specific, and its objectives are vastly more ambitious and more contestable.

A minimalist constitution will require more interpretive work than more routine legal instruments. Indeed, it will not work without judicially supplied doctrines that translate the text and structure into institutional practice. There is no separation of powers rule in the Constitution; instead, there is a (complicated, evolving) separation of powers *doctrine*. There is no federalism rule in the Constitution; what we have, to make sense of the Constitution, is a federalism *doctrine* (actually, an entire web of interrelated doctrines). "Freedom of speech" is a web of *doctrines* on obscenity, truthful advertising, campaign finance, and so on. The doctrines will change (and have changed) over time. They must adapt the Constitution to changing or unforeseen circumstances—"the varying crises of human affairs," in Marshall's words. However, the Constitution itself remains unchanged.

Further, the Constitution's ambition to order political life for posterity means that it requires some coherent theory of what the instrument is supposed to do. John Marshall called this the "genius" of the Constitution (see box 8). You cannot get that genius from the text or history alone; it requires a deeper understanding. There will be more than one plausible account of the Constitution's genius, and people will disagree even if they all agree that the Constitution must be enforced "to the letter." In this important sense, there is no single "right" constitution beyond politics, only better and worse theories. Constitutional argument is always legal *and* political. John Marshall was a great jurist *and* statesman. The Supreme Court is a court *and* a political institution—a branch of government.

Box 8: The Genius of the Constitution

The need to elucidate the Constitution's genius arises, most obviously, over grand moral questions: does "equal protection" permit affirmative action for racial minorities? Does it include women? Gays? Taxpayers? Corporations? But it also arises over humdrum matters. Suppose Illinois were to grant United Airlines a monopoly over flights into and out of O'Hare: can it do that?

The Constitution empowers Congress to prohibit the scheme under its power to regulate "commerce among the several states." But suppose Congress sits on its hands: does the Constitution of its own force block the Illinois law? (Don't go looking for a constitutional clause: there isn't any.) You can argue that the Constitution meant to leave states free to provide for their citizens' welfare as the states see fit and until and unless Congress says otherwise. Or you can argue that the Constitution meant to block state interferences with interstate commerce. To some degree, the Constitution embodies both objectives; how do they fit together? You will need a doctrine that governs this and similar cases, and that doctrine will have to rest on the Constitution's general purposes and "genius."

John Marshall tackled the state monopoly problem in *Gibbons v. Ogden* (1824). Are you persuaded by his answer and arguments?

THE LIVING CONSTITUTION AND ITS ORIGINALIST ENEMIES

Marshall's understanding of constitutionalism remained common ground throughout the nineteenth century. Beginning in the early twentieth century, however, it came under vehement attack by proponents of a "Living Constitution," who argued that the classical understanding blocked the Constitution's adaptation to profound social and economic changes that the founders had not remotely envisioned: industrial capitalism; labor unions; massive social dislocations and demands for redistribution; an emergent administrative state; mass democracy; and organized political parties vying to accommodate urgent social demands.

"Progressive" and, in the 1930s, New Deal politicians and advocates argued that a century-old instrument, crafted by upper-class members of an agrarian society of some 4 million people, ought to give way to modern democratic demands and social imperatives.

The Living Constitution has remained the liberal-progressive program to this day. Its institutional orientation, however, has changed. Its original thrust was directed against the Supreme Court and its allegedly outdated view of the Constitution; the point was to create more room for democratic politics. After the New Deal had triumphed, and with the advent of the Warren Court in the 1950s and the civil rights revolution in the 1950s and 1960s, the once-loathed Supreme Court became identified with the Living Constitution. In the modern progressive view, the Court's duty is to update the Constitution in light of social demands and moral aspirations that are widely shared but all too often frustrated in the political process.

This "activist" judicial role of the Court—on display in countless cases over the rights of criminal defendants, the death penalty, school integration, abortion, and other intensely controversial issues—produced a backlash. Beginning with Richard M. Nixon in 1968, Republican presidential contenders promised to appoint judges and justices who would exercise "deference" to political institutions and "strict" constitutional construction. In the 1980s, conservative theorists reformulated this position into a more ambitious theory of "originalism." The text of the Constitution, they insist, must be understood in the sense of its "public meaning" at the time of its enactment.

Both sides to this controversy hold some attraction. Both, however, also confront difficulties. Living constitutionalists must explain why we should trust an unelected, elitist judiciary to update the document. Originalists, for their part, must explain why we should consider ourselves bound by an ancient text and what we should do about deeply entrenched institutional practices that manifestly depart from that text (for example, the administrative state). Both sides have invested great effort and ingenuity in defending and refining their respective positions. In following the intense and often sophisticated and nuanced debate, bear in mind that the contending theories owe their origins and commitments not to some transcendent constitutional truth but to historical circumstances and intensely political, ideological demands, which the combatants often fail to articulate.

11

CONCLUSION: CONSTITUTIONALISM IN OUR TIME

This book has provided an introduction to constitutional theory—emphasis on *introduction*. You may be disappointed at its lack of answers to many of the questions that agitate our politics: Is there a constitutional right to gay marriage? Should we have a balanced budget amendment? Was the Supreme Court right or wrong in *Bush* v. *Gore* (2000) or in the "Obamacare" case? Questions of this sort matter greatly, and I trust that you will have time and occasion to examine them. My hope is that you will approach them in a broader frame of mind—beyond political slogans and partisan commitments and with a heightened sense of their context and implications. Two concluding thoughts suggest some of the broad questions that arise frequently in our contemporary debate.

CONSTITUTIONAL ARGUMENT

Constitutional argument and debate are all around us—in the newspapers, on campus, at the office water cooler and our dinner tables. Do not take the pervasiveness of constitutional debate for granted: it is an exceptional feature of American politics. Moreover, it is a constitutionally intended feature.

Our constitution is not a sacred text entrusted to experts or oracles. It states no moral principles on which our betters could claim any special authority. Rather, in words that are intelligible to all, it

"*Our constitution is not a sacred text entrusted to experts or oracles. It states no moral principles on which our betters could claim any special authority. Rather, in words that are intelligible to all, it establishes rival, competing institutions—all eager to have their way, all insistent on the democratic and constitutional legitimacy, as well as the wisdom and utility, of their cause.*"

establishes rival, competing institutions—all eager to have their way, all insistent on the democratic and constitutional legitimacy, as well as the wisdom and utility, of their cause. Different institutions will attract different political constituencies. They all have self-serving motives, and they all claim the mantle of the Constitution. The debate is often rancorous and at times seems pointless or even frivolous. Must we *really* have a debate over the meaning of "commerce" in the Constitution before we get on with providing reliable health insurance? Why do partisans on all sides always have to press the Constitution into service? Shouldn't we be more principled about the Constitution?

Yes and no. Of course, constitutional debate requires a certain amount of candor, good faith, and intellectual honesty. Still, pure principles are for philosophers, not for citizens and their politics. The genius of our constitution is to connect politics and principle. Its structural features (such as minimalism and competition) invite argument and so "politicize" our constitution. But in the process, they also democratize constitutional debate and constitutionalize our politics.

For this reason, every major political debate in American history has also been a constitutional debate. Such debates surrounded practices and institutions that now strike us as unproblematic and indeed admirable, from the income tax to Social Security to the Civil Rights Act. In retrospect the debates often seem silly. (Who would think of running a big country *without* an income tax?) However, they arose over very big innovations in American politics and government. Constitutional debate is a way of ensuring that in undertaking grand new experiments, we remain true to our principles and traditions. Constitutional disagreement is no sign of impending collapse or disintegration, at least not necessarily. More often, it is a sign of a healthy constitutional democracy, and not a bad way of running a free country.

MADISONIAN THEORY, THEN AND NOW

Rising economic inequality, recurrent financial crises, mounting public debts, political polarization, and the inability of our political system to respond promptly and effectively to those challenges have caused public disaffection and concern, bordering on alarm. Could it be that our constitutional system, after many permutations and under very different circumstances, has become a cause of those difficulties or an impediment to their solution? Ordinary politics, the founders believed, will operate tolerably well because the Constitution provides sensible, competitive institutional ground rules. It is legitimate and indeed urgent to ask whether that confidence is still warranted.

Madison's great fear, recall, was *majority* faction. Nowadays, we are far more worried about the ability of small, "special" interests to exploit a large, underinformed majority. (Think of agricultural subsidies or of tax "loopholes" that benefit a handful of hedge fund managers.) Madison's comforting assurance that majority coalitions would usually be formed on principles of "justice and the general good" fails to take account of legislative logrolling, to the point where entire statutes, running hundreds of pages in length, consist of interest group favors. Madison's *Federalist* 62 contains a grim indictment of public "instability" and of a "mutable government."

Read it: our own mutable government looks like Madison's nightmare.

Similarly, Madison's theory assumes that one can endow institutions with *permanent* rivalrous ambitions. It also recognizes, however, that the accomplishment of public purposes requires institutional cooperation; and the power to cooperate is the power to collude. Our federalism and administrative state, we have seen, can be viewed as forms of collusion, calculated to evade political responsibility and public accountability. More and more, government power oozes from impenetrable intergovernmental bureaucracies.

Concerns of this sort are not entirely new. Robert McIlwain, an illustrious British scholar then lecturing at Harvard, expressed many of them in a brilliant 1947 treatise entitled *Constitutionalism, Ancient and Modern*. Constitutional checks and balances, he argued, will draw interests into their orbit. The dynamic will soon corrupt and immobilize government and erode its liberal, constitutional foundations. Constitutionalism's true defense, McIlwain urged, is a constitutional "higher law," safeguarded by a suitably educated legal elite.

Decades later, McIlwain's argument resonates. The founders supposed that government, and the federal government in particular, would not try to do too much. Now, in contrast, government programs cover and shape every aspect of citizens' livelihoods—the labor market, health care and insurance, retirement benefits, education, and much else besides. Under such circumstances, it becomes hard to sustain confidence in competitive politics: too much, it appears, is at stake. Perhaps for this reason, liberal democracies, including ours, have tended to transfer power over important matters to unelected, "independent" bodies— market regulation, to agencies; money, to central banks; values decisions, to the courts.

It is difficult to see, though, how this can work in the long run. The judiciary's higher-law authority lasts so long as the higher law itself has a widely shared basis. However, it has become, if anything, *more* ideological, unsettled, and unsettling than our ordinary politics. Does the higher law command free markets or redistribution? Does it forbid or require affirmative action? Gay marriage, polygamy, or "traditional" marriage? Abortion? McIlwain's notion that a well-trained legal establishment could check the ideological tendencies of our politics seems illusory.

And so it ends: an introduction to constitutional theory has left you with troublesome questions about the state of our politics. The answers, if any are to be had, must be sought in the deep reservoir of our constitutional thought and traditions. That reservoir does not replenish itself. Now as always, the task requires our thoughtful attention and active engagement.

**RECOMMENDED
READING**

Students who wish to explore the United States Constitution more extensively and deeply than I have attempted in this book will find the sheer amount of literature and information overwhelming. My own principal contribution [Michael S. Greve, *The Upside-Down Constitution* (Cambridge, MA: Harvard University Press, 2012)], is not a good way to pursue further study; it is written for a professional audience. It is much better to begin with the foundational texts and standard works. My list of recommendations includes many titles that you would find on any scholar's list, along with some more idiosyncratic selections with bearing on the questions covered in this book.

BOOKS

The Founding

The "must read" is *The Federalist*, available in numerous serviceable editions. Far and away the best commentary is David F. Epstein, *The Political Theory of the Federalist* (Chicago: University of Chicago Press, 1984). The standard collection of the Antifederalists' writings is Herbert Storing, ed., *The Complete Anti-Federalist* (Chicago: University of Chicago Press, 1981); among many useful compilations of the principal essays is W. B. Allen and Gordon Lloyd, eds., *The Essential Antifederalist*, 2nd ed. (Lanham, MD: Rowman & Littlefield, 2002). James Madison's and others' notes on the Constitutional Convention—indispensable to understanding the Constitution's drafting—are collected in Max Farrand, ed., *The Records of the Federal Convention of 1787* (New Haven, CT: Yale University Press, 1911); also available online from the

Liberty Fund at http://oll.libertyfund.org/?option=com_staticxt&staticfile=show.php%3Ftitle=1785&Itemid=27).

Among the hundreds of books on the founding, two brilliant works might prove particularly helpful in deepening your understanding: Ahkil Reed Amar, *America's Constitution: A Biography* (New York: Random House Trade Paperbacks, 2006); and Jack N. Rakove, *Original Meanings: Politics and Ideas in the Making of the Constitution* (New York: Knopf, 1996).

Commentary; Constitutional Law

In the union's early decades, collections of judicial cases were haphazard; magisterial "commentaries" played an enormous role in shaping lawyers' and judges' understanding of the Constitution. The most important of these were the *Commentaries on the Constitution of the United States* (1833), by Joseph Story. The youngest justice ever to be appointed to the Supreme Court (at age 32, in 1811) and, next to John Marshall, the greatest jurist in our history, Story published (in 1840) an abridged version called *A Familiar Exposition of the Constitution of the United States* (Lake Bluff, IL: Regnery Gateway, 2000). It is a brilliant clause-by-clause exposition of the Constitution and its purposes.

The Founders' Constitution, ed. Philip Kurland and Ralph Lerner (University of Chicago Press and the Liberty Fund, 2000), http://press-pubs.uchicago.edu/founders/, is an indispensable reference work. Clause by constitutional clause, it provides background information, excerpts from the debates at the Constitutional Convention, excerpts of early Supreme Court decisions, and additional authoritative materials.

Nowadays, constitutional law is taught from casebooks, which you will find in any law library. They are useful in finding competently edited Supreme Court decisions in major cases. However, because they are designed to drum cases into law students' heads, they tend to confuse the Supreme Court's pronouncements with the actual Constitution. The exception is Michael Stokes Paulsen et al., *The Constitution of the United States* (New York: Foundation Press, 2010). Excerpts from major cases are accompanied by historical materials and extensive editors' notes that put the cases in context.

Constitutional Theory

For a deep, substantive engagement with constitutionalism, I recommend two difficult, controversial, but immensely rewarding books: Bruce Ackerman, *We the People: Foundations* (Cambridge, MA: Harvard University Press, 1991); and Charles McIlwain, *Constitutionalism: Ancient and Modern* (Ithaca, NY: Cornell University Press, 1947).

Contemporary theorists have reformulated the Constitution's Lockean and Madisonian foundations in intriguing ways. These works, too, are difficult, but they may hold great reward for students with an interest in economics or political economy. The "must read" is James M. Buchanan and Gordon Tullock, *The Calculus of Consent: Logical Foundations of Constitutional Democracy*

(Ann Arbor: University of Michigan Press, 1962), in many ways, the foundation of all modern constitutional theory. A very fine "neo-Madisonian," game-theoretic account of how constitutions (and ours in particular) work is Robert D. Cooter, *The Strategic Constitution* (Princeton, NJ: Princeton University Press, 2000).

The Supreme Court

The fundamental point to comprehend is that the Supreme Court is both a court and a political agent—a branch of government. The origin of that insight, and still the best source to explore it, is Robert G. McCloskey, *The American Supreme Court* (Chicago: University of Chicago Press, 2004). Like McCloskey, Barry Friedman, *The Will of the People* (New York: Farrar, Straus and Giroux, 2009), argues that the Supreme Court will over the long haul follow public sentiments. The author's theory is not free from doubt. However, the book provides a fascinating and reliable account of the Supreme Court in the context of public opinion over the course of our history. The footnotes are a very good place to begin a research or paper assignment on the major cases and controversies in Supreme Court history.

ONLINE RESOURCES

The Internet provides an enormous wealth of information on the U.S. Constitution and its history. The Law Library of Congress (www.loc.gov/law/help/guide/federal/usconst.php) offers a straightforward guide to key constitutional documents. The National Constitution Center (http://ratify.constitutioncenter.org/constitution/) is particularly helpful for students seeking to find information on specific sections of the Constitution. (It allows viewers to search by keyword or topic and to browse through Supreme Court cases.)

The Avalon Project at Yale Law School (http://avalon.law.yale.edu/subject_menus/constpap.asp), is an excellent source of primary materials, including documents from the Constitutional Convention and prior works that influenced and inspired the Constitution. The Heritage Foundation's Guide to the Constitution (www.heritage.org/constitution) offers a detailed, clause-by-clause analysis of the Constitution, written by prominent scholars. Heritage is a staunchly conservative organization, and its site is explicitly devoted to an originalist understanding of the Constitution. However, it is commendably free from ideological bias.

For students with an interest in other countries' constitutions, HeinOnline (http://heinonline.org/HeinDocs/WorldConstitutionsIllustrated.pdf) provides a current constitution for every country in the world, along with historical documents.

ABOUT THE AUTHOR

Michael S. Greve is a professor at George Mason University School of Law. From 2000 to August 2012, he was the John G. Searle Scholar at the American Enterprise Institute, where he remains a visiting scholar. Before coming to AEI, Greve cofounded and, from 1989 to 2000, directed the Center for Individual Rights, a public interest law firm. Currently, he also chairs the board of the Competitive Enterprise Institute and is a frequent contributor to the Liberty Law Blog.

Greve has written extensively on many aspects of the American legal system. His publications include numerous law review articles and books, including most recently *The Upside-Down Constitution* (2012). He has also written *The Demise of Environmentalism in American Law* (1996); *Real Federalism: Why It Matters, How It Could Happen* (1999); and *Harm-less Lawsuits? What's Wrong With Consumer Class Actions* (2005). He is the coeditor, with Richard A. Epstein, of *Competition Laws in Conflict: Antitrust Jurisdiction in the Global Economy* (2004) and *Federal Preemption: States' Powers, National Interests* (2007); and, with Michael Zoeller, of *Citizenship in America and Europe: Beyond the Nation-State?* (2009).